AR7.0
1 pt.

W9-DJP-990

Weight-Loss Programs: Weighing the Risks and Realities

Weight-Loss Programs:

Weighing the Risks and Realities

Michele Ingber Drohan

THE ROSEN PUBLISHING GROUP, INC.
NEW YORK

The Teen Health
Library of
Eating Disorder
Prevention

To my parents, who have always been there for me.

The people pictured in this book are only models. They in no way practice or endorse the activities illustrated. Captions serve only to explain the subjects of photographs and do not in any way imply a connection between the real-life models and the staged situations. News agency photos are exceptions.

Published in 1998 by the Rosen Publishing Group, Inc.
29 East 21st Street, New York, NY 10010

Library of Congress Cataloging-in-Publication Data

Drohan, Michele Ingber.
    Weight-loss programs : weighing the risks and realities / Michele Ingber Drohan. -- 1st ed.
    p. cm. -- (The teen health library of eating disorder prevention)
    Includes bibliographical references and index.
    Summary: Discusses the relationship between health and diet and examines a variety of commercial weight-loss programs and the health risks that they pose to their members.
    ISBN 0-8239-2770-9
    1. Eating disorders in adolescence--Treatment--Juvenile literature. 2. Weight loss--Juvenile literature. 3. Reducing diets--Juvenile literature. 4. Body image--Juvenile literature. 5. Obesity in adolescence--Juvenile literature. 6. Teenagers--Nutrition--Juvenile literature. 7. Self-esteem--Juvenile literature. [1. Weight loss. 2. Reducing diets. 3. Eating disorders. 4. Body image.] I. Title. II. Series.
RJ506.E18D76 1998
616.85'26'00835--dc21   98-4418
                                                            CIP
                                                            AC

Manufactured in the United States of America

Contents

Introduction

"If I were thinner, I know I'd have a boyfriend."

"Every time I have a snack, my brother and his friends make jokes about my weight."

"I can't believe I ate that pizza tonight! Now I'll never fit into that new pair of jeans. I'm such a pig."

Does this sound like you? How often do you think about your weight or wish that you were thinner? How do you feel about yourself when you do think about it?

Unfortunately, many people equate their worth as a person with how much they weigh. In our society, you are often told that being thin means being happy and successful. You can find this idea everywhere you look—television, movies, and magazines. In response, many people go on diets to try to lose weight. According to studies by Eating Disorders Awareness Prevention, Inc. (EDAP), 80

Popular culture, shown in magazines, on television, and in movies, often equates thinness with happiness and success.

percent of ten-year-old girls in the United States have already been on a diet at some point in their young lives.

Because of our culture's obsession with losing weight, there are countless products and programs that claim to want to help you become a thinner and happier person. These weight-loss programs reinforce the idea that the only way to be happy is to be slim—and you can't do it without them. Look through any magazine, or turn on the television and you will most likely find an advertisement for a weight-loss program. They make promises and guarantees—"Lose five pounds in five days!"

What these ads don't tell you is that, for most people, trying to reach this cultural ideal is unrealistic, often impossible, and sometimes dangerous. They don't tell you about the dangers of diets, and that, ultimately, diets don't work. Instead they say that dieting is the answer to your "problem" and that being thin is what matters most.

This book will discuss the realities of weight-loss programs. It will explain what happens when you enter a program, and help you understand the information you are given. It will also tell you about the physical, emotional, and financial costs of dieting.

Overall, you'll learn why weight isn't as important as you may think. If you've ever been on a diet or you're thinking about joining a weight-loss program, this book will give you the facts you need to make a smart decision. Then you can choose for yourself what's right for you. Hopefully, you'll decide to work toward accepting your body and living a healthy lifestyle. This book will help you do that, too.

What Is a Weight-Loss Program?

According to the Diet Business Bulletin, there are approximately 10,000 weight-loss centers in the United States. The most well-known are Weight Watchers, Jenny Craig, and Nutri/System. Most likely, you've heard of one, or even all three of them. Maybe you've even joined one of them already. Since Weight Watchers started in 1962, more than 25 million people have joined it—some even more than once.

Although the details of each program may differ, all weight-loss programs aim to do one thing: to put you on a diet and to help you lose weight.

Considering that

many people want to lose weight, you may think that there's nothing wrong with helping people do just that. You may ask, "What's wrong with supporting someone who wants to shed a few pounds?" When weight-loss programs tell you that losing weight will make you healthier and happier, it sounds like a great idea. But it's important to listen closely to what these programs offer—and to hear what they're really designed to do.

Joining a Program

Many programs offer a free consultation if you're interested in joining; they will give you information and help you decide if their programs are right for you. You will sit down with a trained counselor to discuss weight and weight-loss goals. The counselor should have a background in nutrition and exercise, as well as psychology.

The first thing a counselor will do is weigh you, then tell you what your ideal weight should be. Depending on how much weight you want to lose, or how much a counselor recommends you lose, you are given a time frame for your weight-loss goal. This is sometimes referred to as a "personal goal weight." You may not have a say in what kind of program the counselor selects for you. You tell the counselor your goal and he or she will pick a plan for you. The counselor will tell you that you need to follow the plan exactly if you want to achieve your goal weight.

A counselor will also tell you that the rate of your weight loss is directly connected with how well you follow the program. Many programs claim that you will lose between one and two pounds each week. Counselors suggest that you stay on the program until you learn how to keep the weight off on your own. This could take from six months to a year or longer.

There are often no criteria for anyone interested in joining a weight-loss program. They will accept someone who is five pounds overweight or someone who is fifty pounds overweight. All you need is a desire to lose weight.

Signing Up

After you and your counselor decide on a plan, it's time to sign up for the program officially. This usually involves paying a membership fee and scheduling counseling sessions. With Weight Watchers, for instance, you pay a registration fee and a weekly fee at the first meeting. You'll continue to pay per *meeting*. To keep your membership valid, you must pay the fee each week, whether or not you attend the meeting. If you miss one or two meetings, you must pay for them at the next meeting you attend. The membership becomes invalid after six consecutive weeks of absences. You can rejoin at any time, but must pay the same cost as new members.

Membership fees will vary depending on where you live and how long you decide to stay on the weight-loss program.

In New York, for example, it can cost around $100 for a full-year membership to Jenny Craig. Weight Watchers lets you pay a monthly fee of between $10 and $14. Nutri/System, on the other hand, may charge you up to $100 for just one month. And, these membership fees do not include the cost of food.

Before you join a program ask about its refund policy if you decide to quit in the middle of it. With Weight Watchers, you pay as you

Weight-loss programs often encourage you to purchase pre-packaged foods specially designed for dieters. Eating these foods regularly can become very expensive.

go along, but with other programs where you prepay, you may not get your money refunded.

Depending on the program and your age, you may have to bring a parent along with you to join. Jenny Craig, in particular, has a special adolescent program that requires parental approval if you are under the legal age, which is eighteen years old in most states.

Food

The major programs, such as Jenny Craig, Weight Watchers, and Nutri/System, offer their own pre-packaged food. Whether you have to buy the food depends on the program. Nutri/System's focus is on food, so purchasing it is essential. In addition to the membership fees, the food can cost up to $49 each week. Jenny Craig programs also require that you buy their food, which runs about $70-$100 each week. Weight Watchers programs give you the option of buying their food, which can be found in most grocery stores.

Weight-loss programs will always recommend that you buy their food. They'll tell you that purchasing their food will give you a better chance of reaching your goal. Your recommended food plan is very specific and often "portion-controlled." This means no matter what type of food they tell you to eat, you can eat only so much of it.

When participating in a plan that includes the program's food, you often are not supposed to eat out. If

Many weight-loss programs will tell you that your success in losing weight depends on how strictly you follow their program.

you do go out to eat, some programs give you tips for ordering food in a restaurant so you don't break the diet. But other programs are extremely rigid about the food and will not allow this, especially in the first few weeks of the program. This can make spending time socializing with family and friends very difficult.

Counseling Sessions

You will also attend a counseling session each week to check your progress during the diet program. At the counseling session, you will review the program's diet restrictions. Some programs offer individual and group support sessions. You are weighed at every session. Your success in reaching your goal is measured by the number on the scale. You can also attend group meetings, where people encourage and support each other through the program.

Once you've reached your goal weight, the program offers you a maintenance program to help you keep the weight off. This may take the form of more counseling sessions or additional materials provided by the program. The cost for these counseling sessions varies depending on where you live and what program you join.

What's the Problem?

Dana was really excited when she signed up with Jenny Craig. She wanted to lose weight before she started school in September. She imagined the surprise on her friends' faces when she showed up on the first day of school with her thin body. Dana had saved up money from her summer job as a lifeguard to pay for the sessions. With her mom's approval she joined.

The counselor at the program recommended a 1,000-calorie-per-day diet. During the first week she ate the program's food that consisted of pre-packaged dinners and artificially flavored chocolate snacks. She also drank lots of water. But it wasn't enough. She felt tired and moody. Being a lifeguard required her to get up early and be active and alert all day.

When she went back the next week, she told her counselor that she needed more food to get through the day. But the counselor told her that if she really wanted to lose weight, she had to stick to the diet. After three weeks, Dana quit. She felt like a complete failure.

Dana is not alone. Many people join and rejoin weight-loss programs, often feeling like a bad person if they can't stick to their diets or if they gain back their weight. The weight-loss centers would like you to believe that it's your fault if you quit the program or regain the pounds you've lost. But there's actually a lot more to consider.

The Truth About Weight-Loss Programs

Weight-loss programs are a business like any other. That means they need to make a profit to succeed. As a result, the companies and their staffs are motivated to make money. To do so, various weight-loss centers, such as Nutri/System and Jenny Craig, arranged to make drugs like fen-phen and Redux available to their clients in addition to their existing diet and exercise programs. In 1995, when Nutri/System needed to emerge from bankruptcy protection, it made prescription diet pills, such as Redux and fen-phen, available to clients in addition to its diet program.

Medical experts worried about the risks of these pills, as well as the way in which they were prescribed. The pills were meant for people who were fifteen to twenty pounds overweight or more. But many women who wanted to lose only a few pounds were taking the pills.

The pills became very easy to get, and they caused many health problems for users. They were available in many of the weight-loss programs. Doctors, some of whom worked for weight-loss centers, wrote 18 million prescriptions for these pills in 1997 alone.

Redux is the brand name for dexfenfluramine. Fen-phen is a combination of two drugs: fenfluramine and an amphetamine-like drug called phentermine. These drugs were approved by the Food and Drug Administration (FDA). The FDA is responsible for testing and approving all drugs for safety before they are sold to consumers. But as more and more people used the drugs, some started experiencing side effects. The drugs were discovered to cause serious health problems for some users.

One reported problem is a rare lung disease that is often fatal. The FDA also received reports about harmful side effects from Redux, including eighteen deaths and twenty-six psychotic episodes (periods of severe anger and aggression). Some programs, like Jenny

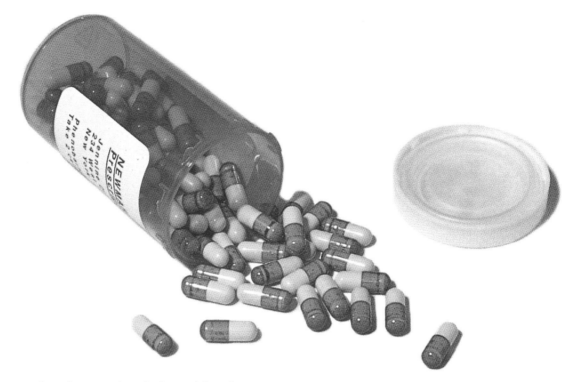

Diet drugs, such as Redux and fen-phen, are dangerous and can cause serious health problems.

Craig, decided to stop making prescription diet pills available to their clients until further studies were done to test the drugs' safety.

In September, 1997, the FDA decided that the diet drugs could be dangerous and asked the drug manufacturers to pull them off the market. The drugs caused serious heart problems in 30 percent of the people who took them. Some companies, however, didn't stop making them available until they were forced to stop by the FDA.

No two weight-loss programs are identical. However, you've learned what commonly happens when a person joins a weight-loss program. Now let's take a look at each of the factors involved.

Counselors: Friends or Foes?

While it may seem that the counselors at weight-loss programs are there to support you, they are often motivated by something else. At most programs, the counselors are paid around $5-$10 an hour. Most of their income comes from commissions. This means they earn a certain percentage of money depending on how much they sell. The more they sell, the more money they make. The commissions come from sales of the pre-packaged food and other supplementary materials, such as guidebooks, cookbooks, and vitamins, that they recommend to you.

The counselors who work at these programs are not medical doctors. They don't know your medical history. A program counselor should tell you up front to visit a doctor

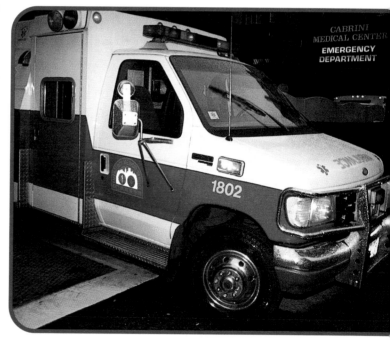

Weight-loss counselors are not medically trained. They cannot assess the medical or health risks of weight loss in the way that a doctor can.

before you enter the program. A doctor can decide if the program is right for you.

Most of the programs don't require that you go to a doctor for a medical exam, however, and don't check to see if you've recently seen a doctor or not. The programs are supposed to watch for clients who have or have had eating disorders. But when it comes to signing up a new client, a counselor may not ask you the right questions.

Success Rates

All weight-loss programs claim that if you stick with their diets, you will lose weight—and keep it off. If you ask counselors about the success rate of their programs, most will tell you that his or her program is more successful than any other. But if you ask for proof, you'll find there are no statistics to back up their claims. It would make sense for a weight-loss program to track the success of its clients. What better way to advertise the program and prove to potential clients that the program works? But neither Weight Watchers nor Nutri/System has any published reports on their success rates.

In 1993, *Consumer Reports* surveyed 19,000 readers who had tried a weight-loss program. The survey showed that more than two-thirds of the dieters had gained back the weight they lost within two years after leaving the program.

In the end, it seems that the most successful clients are those who work for the company. In those cases, a person would have to dedicate his or her life to dieting. But no counselor working at a weight-loss program will tell you that when you sign up. Instead most will tell you that if you regain the weight, it's because you lack the willpower or the desire to really lose the weight. Ultimately, they may claim it's your fault, not the program's, that you were unable to keep off the weight.

Your "Ideal" Weight: Fact or Fiction?

Most programs use a chart to calculate your healthy weight range. The chart created by the Metropolitan Life Insurance Company has been considered the standard for determining a healthy weight range. You may be familiar with it. While a weight-loss program may encourage you

Experts are reevaluating their ideas about an "ideal" weight.

to choose a goal that is realistic for you, many leading experts question the way in which they measure your health.

Most weight-loss programs will tell you that extra weight is a serious health problem. They claim that being overweight can increase a person's chances of developing diabetes, high blood pressure, a heart condition, and some forms of cancer. Therefore, they say, it's necessary to figure out what your ideal weight should be, and work toward it. This will improve your physical well-being.

This thinking, however, has been seriously challenged. In 1992, the National Institute of Health (NIH) gathered a panel of researchers who specialized in obesity, nutrition, health, and exercise. The purpose of the conference was to find out if dieting worked, and if it was healthy and safe. What they discovered was that losing weight by dieting alone won't automatically make a person healthier. They decided that more research needs to be done on what makes a person healthy.

In 1995, the government adjusted its chart for weight formulas in its *Dietary Guidelines for Americans*. While this chart is more flexible, many experts don't believe in using weight charts. In general, charts don't account for many different, important factors, like bone mass, muscle mass, and age.

Individual Set Point

There is strong evidence to support that people have their own individual set point of weight. It varies from person to person, much like hair color or eye color. This set point is 80 percent genetic. Your body shape and size are established mainly by the shape and size of your parents' bodies. This means that you have only so much control over how much you weigh and what your body looks like.

Many experts are beginning to believe that your weight doesn't matter as much as your overall health. How healthy you are depends more on how much you exercise than on how much you weigh. A person who is 5′2″ at 140 pounds and who exercises and eats healthful foods can be just as healthy, if not healthier, than a 5′2″ person who weighs 110 pounds, but never exercises and eats candy bars for lunch. It's not fatness that matters, it's fitness.

A study of 25,000 men at the Cooper Institute for Aerobic Research in Dallas found that "those who were more fit had lower death rates—even if they were overweight." Scientists have also realized that where fat is located on your body makes a difference. If the fat is in a person's stomach area, the health risk is greater than if the fat lies around the hips and thighs.

Another study from the National Institute on Aging found that "the lowest mortality rates are associated with people who gain modest amounts of weight during adulthood. Gaining a great deal of weight contributes to earlier mortality—but so does losing weight." These kinds of studies clearly show that simply losing weight isn't always the answer.

Money

It costs a lot of money to join a weight-loss program—as much as hundreds of dollars each month. In addition to the membership fees, there also are pre-pack-

To be healthy, exercise is usually more important than weight.

aged foods to consider, as well as vitamin supplements and various maintenance programs. A weight-loss program tells you that you need it to teach you how to live a healthy lifestyle. But it will charge you money to learn.

Information on living a healthy lifestyle is actually available in many other places for free. You can do your own research on what kinds of foods are good for you. Take a look at the USDA Food Guide Pyramid. It tells you everything you need to know about the four basic food groups. You can talk to health professionals and read books on nutrition from your local bookstore or library.

The biggest problem with weight-loss programs, though, is that you can spend all that money and learn an unrealistic way to live and eat. In the following chapter, you'll read about how your body reacts, both physically and psychologically, when you go on a diet.

Why Diets Don't Work

3

Most of you probably don't think about control when it comes to food. When you're hungry, you eat what you want. Sometimes it may be something healthful—other times, you may give in to your craving for some chocolate, potato chips, or a burger. Whatever you decide, you usually control what you eat or don't eat. But when you join a weight-loss program, that control is taken away from you. The program decides what you eat, when you eat, and how much you eat. When someone else controls the way you eat, it's very natural to rebel. As a result, most people end up breaking the diet they've started. When you don't lose weight, you often blame yourself and feel like a failure. This can lead to depression and a negative body image. It can also lead to unhealthy attitudes toward food. In the end, you could end up feeling more obsessed with food and weight loss than ever before.

The most common practice in all weight-loss programs is the "weigh-in." Every time you meet with a counselor, or attend a meeting, you get on the scale to check if you've lost weight. And each time the number decreases, you are rewarded. Some Weight Watchers groups even hand out gold stars to people who have lost certain amounts. If you're one of these people, you will feel like a good person. If you are in a group meeting, everyone claps and cheers at the weight you've lost. If you don't lose weight, you may still receive support from the program. However, because so much emphasis is placed on the weight loss, you might feel like a failure or a "bad" person inside.

Because of this emphasis on a goal weight, many people who diet become too focused on a number. Eventually they think of themselves only in terms of

By placing too much emphasis on weight, you may forget important things such as eating a balanced diet, living a healthy lifestyle, and appreciating your inner self.

their weight. They may forget that there are many qualities that define a person. Qualities like intelligence, a sense of humor, honesty, and generosity may become less important compared to how much a person weighs and what a person looks like. When all you think about is food and weight, you have less time for more meaningful things in your life.

The Physical Consequences of Dieting

Your body converts the food you eat into energy. This energy keeps your body going. Your body needs food to survive. When your body does not receive the necessary amount of food it needs to carry on its normal functions, it responds as if it is being attacked. When it doesn't get what it needs, it tries to defend itself. Your body is very good at making the necessary adjustments.

As you learned in the last chapter, everyone has an individual set-point weight, which is determined mostly by genetics. When your body dips below its set point (by skipping meals or restricting calories), it reacts by lowering its metabolism. Metabolism is the rate at which the body burns calories. When your metabolism is lowered, your body stores fat more efficiently. This means as you eat less, your body makes up for the loss by holding on to that food to survive. As a result, when a person diets for a period of time, and then goes off the diet, his or her body usually gains back more weight. This is because your metabolism rate doesn't return to normal even after you stop dieting.

"My diet only allowed me an orange and a chocolate drink for breakfast. By the time I got to school, I felt weak and dizzy."

While weight-loss programs claim that being overweight can cause health problems, there is strong evidence that shows the negative effects of dieting.

Dieting is actually the main cause of many physical problems. Lack of food can cause a drop in blood sugar, which makes you feel light-headed and tired. You might also experience nausea and stomach pains. In addition to these effects, you may develop serious conditions, such as kidney, heart, and liver problems. Your teenage years are a time of growth and development. You are growing from the body of a child to that of an adult. The body needs energy to make this transformation. If you don't provide the nutrients and vitamins it needs, the body will not develop properly.

For a young woman, a lack of nutrients can cause a delay in her first menstrual period or cause her to stop menstruating. As a result, the lack of estrogen (the hormone that causes menstruation) can lead to a lack of calcium in her body. Osteoporosis (a disease that destroys the bones) could develop.

"The whole time I was on the diet, I felt angry and annoyed. The smallest thing would set me off. I would snap at my friends and family for no reason at all."

When you are ignoring your body's hunger signals and not eating enough food, your body slows down and begins to function at a level that is below normal. This can cause you to become irritable and depressed. This depression can trigger the start of dangerous habits, like binge eating.

A person who binges may be unable to stop eating, even when he or she is full.

Binge eating is when a person eats a large amount of food at one sitting. The person often has no control over his or her eating. A binge can happen when a person is on a restrictive diet. He or she can become obsessed with what he or she isn't supposed to eat. When that person reaches the point where he or she can no longer fight the urge to eat, he or she eats without any control or restriction. The person usually can't stop eating, even long after he or she feels full.

This then sets up an unhealthy cycle of yo-yo dieting. Yo-yo dieting is when a person goes on and off a diet

33

several times. After a time, your body, as well as your self-esteem, suffers. You may become more desperate in your quest to lose weight. This quest may involve a number of unhealthy behaviors, such as taking diet pills or laxatives, fasting, and compulsive exercising.

"I found any reason at all to break my diet. If I got a bad grade, or had a fight with my boyfriend, I thought, why bother? I'll eat a pint of ice cream and make it a really bad day."

One damaging factor to dieting is that you may lose the ability to know when you're really hungry. Our stomachs tell us when we're hungry. If you've ever been embarrassed by a grumbling stomach, you know what that means. But when you deny yourself food, you try to ignore those signals. Soon you can't decide when and if you're really hungry anymore. Instead, you might respond to other, external factors that decide when and how much you eat. For example, you might start to eat because you're stressed out or upset. While this happens to everyone sometimes, it's unhealthy when it happens all the time. And when we define ourselves by what we eat, the act of overeating makes us even more depressed.

"I didn't go out to eat with friends or go to parties. I was scared to be around food that wasn't on my diet."

Dieting can teach you to fear food. You may start to divide food into categories of good and bad. You may begin to think of yourself negatively if you eat something "bad." Eventually you stop trusting yourself around food. You can no longer tell when you've had enough to eat. You forget that eating is supposed to be fun and pleasurable. You forget that it's okay to eat something because it tastes good. Food and meals should be positive experiences, often ones that are shared with family and friends. Eating should be enjoyable, not something that makes you feel guilty or like a failure.

Danger!

Most important, however, the dieting attitude can lead someone to develop an eating disorder. Studies show that 80 percent of people who had anorexia or bulimia started with a diet. An eating disorder is extremely damaging and dangerous to a person's health. It can cause major physical and psychological problems in a person's life, and it can even result in death.

What Is an Eating Disorder?

4

When Dawn was thirteen, she went to her family doctor for her yearly check-up. She had gained a few pounds in the last year, and the doctor told her to watch her weight. Dawn responded by exercising and eating low-fat foods. After a few months, she lost weight. Everyone complimented her on how good she looked. Even her parents were proud. Dawn *was very shy and did not have a lot of friends. She liked the attention she was getting. She thought being thinner would make her attractive, popular, and happier. Dawn decided to eat less and exercise more. She measured her food and refused to eat any fat. If she couldn't find the food she wanted, she didn't eat at all.*

When she did eat, she exercised for hours to burn off the calories. She lost more and more weight. Her family became worried about her health. When they tried to talk with her, she refused to listen to them. Dawn was so afraid of gaining weight. She thought everyone was just jealous. Dawn became thinner and thinner, but all she could ever see was a fat person looking back at her in the mirror.

While eating disorders mostly affect females, there is also an increasing number of males who are developing these conditions too. Eating disorders include anorexia nervosa, bulimia nervosa, compulsive exercise, and compulsive eating. A person can suffer from one or any combination of the four disorders. There are certain characteristics of each one, and they all present very dangerous health risks. The reasons why a person, male or female, develops an eating disorder are complex. It's important to realize, however, that when a person develops an eating disorder, food is often not the reason. The person may have psychological problems that show up through the eating disorder.

An eating disorder involves a person's eating habits, his or her attitudes about weight and food, his or her body shape, and other psychological factors. A person suffering from an eating disorder may be experiencing problems in his or her family, job, school, and other relationships. Such people may feel alone and distrustful of others and isolate themselves. They may feel out of control in their lives. Eating disorders are symptoms of these problems. Often, they start as a way for a person to take control over the one thing he or she can—the body.

It's important to understand why and how an eating disorder develops. This way, if you or a friend has an eating disorder, you can help yourself or someone you love. The sooner an eating disorder is identified, the sooner it can be treated.

The major symptoms of anorexia nervosa include:
- Eating very little, or not eating at all
- A severe, illogical fear of fat
- A relentless quest to become thinner
- A distorted body image
- An extreme weight loss

The major symptoms of bulimia nervosa include:
- Binge eating

A person with an eating disorder may have a distorted body image. She may see herself as fat no matter how thin she becomes.

- ❐ Purging, in the form of vomiting, extreme dieting, or an abuse of diet pills and/or laxatives
- ❐ A distorted body image
- ❐ An extreme fear of fat

The major symptoms of compulsive exercise are:
- ❐ Exercising all the time, often in secret
- ❐ A distorted body image
- ❐ An extreme fear of fat
- ❐ Vomiting or an abuse of diet pills and/or laxatives

Compulsive eating is a bit different from the other eating disorders because the person is not trying to lose weight. A person who eats compulsively may eat large amounts of food, but does not try to purge it from his or her body. The person does, however, have an unhealthy relationship with food and needs help. It's also important to note that all the major factors mentioned are not exclusive to only one disorder. In other words, a person with anorexia may abuse diet pills as well. A person with bulimia may be addicted to exercise. A person who suffers from compulsive exercise may also binge.

Finding Help

The following is a list of common signs of eating disorders. You don't need to have all the symptoms on this list to have a problem. The sooner you recognize there is a problem, the sooner you can get help.

Do you:
- ❏ Constantly think about the size and shape of your body?
- ❏ Constantly think about your weight?
- ❏ Constantly think about food and about eating?
- ❏ Continue to diet after you've lost a lot of weight?
- ❏ Not feel good about yourself unless

If you understand how and why an eating disorder develops, you can better help yourself or someone you love.

       you are thin, but never feel satisfied with how thin you are?
- ❏ Feel like you should be exercising even more, no matter how much you are exercising?
- ❏ No longer get your period?
- ❏ Limit the amount and types of foods you eat?
- ❏ Feel competitive about dieting?
- ❏ Force yourself to throw up, or abuse diet pills and/or laxatives?

If any of these sound familiar to you, please get help. Talk with someone you trust—a friend, guidance counselor, teacher, or parent. Always remember that you are not alone and you can recover.

Helping a Friend

You may feel unsure or uncomfortable talking to a friend who you suspect has an eating disorder. Outside of an emergency situation, when help is immediately required because his or her life is in danger, there are some guidelines you can follow in talking with a friend about an eating disorder. It can be difficult because a person with an eating disorder may be extremely reluctant to let go of the behavior, or even admit there's a problem. He or she may become defensive or protective of the dangerous behavior. Usually, eating disorders are a result of someone's trying to control his or her life in the only way possible. Giving up that control isn't easy.

What You Can Do to Help

If you know someone with an eating disorder:

- Set aside some time and talk with your friend privately.
- Talk to your friend in a caring, thoughtful way. Try not to express anger or frustration toward him or her.
- Listen closely to what your friend has to say. Try not to judge what he or she tells you.

- ❏ Don't fight or argue with your friend. If he or she insists there isn't a problem, say that you hope he or she is right, but that you are still concerned.
- ❏ Offer to go with him or her to speak with a counselor or a doctor.
- ❏ Don't try to rescue your friend. You cannot save him or her or force your friend into treatment. All you can do is say that you are concerned. Your friend must be the one to take the first steps toward getting treatment.

Recovering from an eating disorder can be a long and difficult process that involves many steps. A person may be hospitalized or admitted to an in-patient program, where he or she lives for a few months during treatment. Often, individual therapy and group therapy are essential in helping a person recover from an eating disorder.

There are many organizations, support groups, and resources devoted entirely to eating disorder treatment and prevention. Help is available to those who need and want assistance to treat an eating disorder. The road is long, but it's worth it. Many young men and women have recovered. In the end, treatment can save the person's life.

Rebelling Against Diet Culture

5

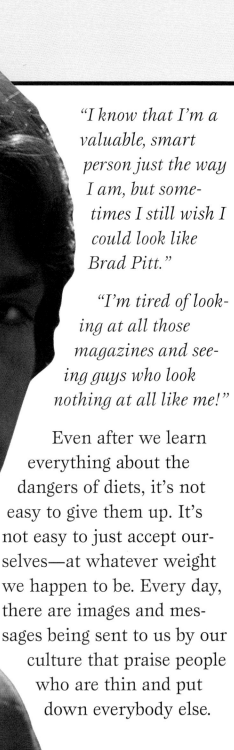

"I know that I'm a valuable, smart person just the way I am, but sometimes I still wish I could look like Brad Pitt."

"I'm tired of looking at all those magazines and seeing guys who look nothing at all like me!"

Even after we learn everything about the dangers of diets, it's not easy to give them up. It's not easy to just accept ourselves—at whatever weight we happen to be. Every day, there are images and messages being sent to us by our culture that praise people who are thin and put down everybody else.

These ideas can be reinforced by our families, our teachers, our doctors, and our friends. Prejudice against overweight people is a very real issue. It's one that won't go away overnight. You are not powerless against it, though. Awareness is the first step. The next thing to do is to try and develop a positive body image for yourself. There are many ways to achieve this. There are also ways to tell the media (newspapers, magazines, television) that you don't like the messages they are sending.

Speak Out

You are a valuable consumer to advertisers. They care about what you think because they want you to buy their products. For example, in a recent column *Seventeen* magazine asked its readers to write and tell them if the fashion models they used were too thin. Many young women reported feeling bad about themselves after they flipped through the latest fashion magazines. *Seventeen* has recognized this and asked their readers to speak out.

In another recent issue, the magazine featured a column by Emme, a popular model for larger-size women and author of *True Beauty*. Emme's book discusses the importance of self-esteem and how everyone should accept different body shapes and sizes. Encouraging letters from readers could make it a regular column. The magazine may not change immediately, but you can use the power you have to urge for more realistic models and for articles about subjects other than beauty and weight-loss.

If you see an advertisement, a movie, a music video, or anything else that you don't like because it encourages the idea that men and women have to be thin in order to be acceptable, speak out. Write a letter to the movie studio or the ad agency and let them know that you don't like the messages they are sending. Organize a campaign, and get everyone to sign a petition. This sends a strong message to the media that you, the consumer, is not happy. They value your opinion, because if you aren't happy, you will not buy their products. This is where you have the greatest power. Your opinion matters, so speak out. Let them know how you feel.

Write It Down

One of the best ways to recognize feelings and notice different moods is to write them down. Writing can be a way to take control over the world around you. For the next month, try to keep a journal about your daily life. Write down a few words after certain events, such as taking a test, going shopping, eating, or exercising. You don't have to write a lot, just jot down how certain moments make you feel. Pay special attention to the next time you pick up the latest fashion magazine, or watch

Writing down your different feelings and moods can help you to recognize and control them.

your favorite television show. What do the women and men look like? Are they realistic representations of your world? Write down how you feel about yourself and your body when you're done reading or watching.

After a month, go back and look over what you wrote. Then try doing some things differently. You can do this by making small changes to avoid the things that make you feel bad. For example, if a magazine depresses you, don't read it anymore. If MTV

47

videos make you feel fat or ugly, turn off the television. Your journal will help you discover the activities that make you feel good about yourself and have a positive impact on your life. If you get mad, write a letter or talk to a close friend about what you think. It takes effort to resist strong cultural messages, but your self-esteem is worth it.

Improving Your Body Image

The following statements have been modified from a list developed by Michael Levine, Ph.D., for the EDAP. These positive statements are meant to promote a positive message. At first, it may be hard to believe or practice some of these messages, but memorize them and repeat them to yourself when you feel bad. After some time, you may find that they can help you to think positively about yourself and your body. They can even help raise your self-esteem and remind you that you are more than just your weight. Share these statements with your close friends. You can say them to yourself or to each other when you need them most:

- ☐ I will remember that being thin will not necessarily make me a happier person.
- ☐ I will stop comparing my body with everyone else's.

- I will do things that make me feel good about myself that don't revolve around my body shape and size.
- I will exercise because it's fun, not because it burns calories.
- I will eat nutritious foods because they taste good and are good for my health, not because they'll help me lose weight.
- I will repeat my good qualities to myself every time I feel like putting myself down.
- I will value other people for who they are, not what they look like.

It isn't easy to develop a positive body image. It takes time. But there are people and organizations who are fighting every day for these messages to be heard and who are working to promote size acceptance. The National Association to Advance Fat Acceptance (NAAFA) works hard to fight prejudice against obesity. Every year it organizes a No Diet Day on May 5. It also accepts anyone as a member— no matter how much they weigh.

Living a Healthy Lifestyle

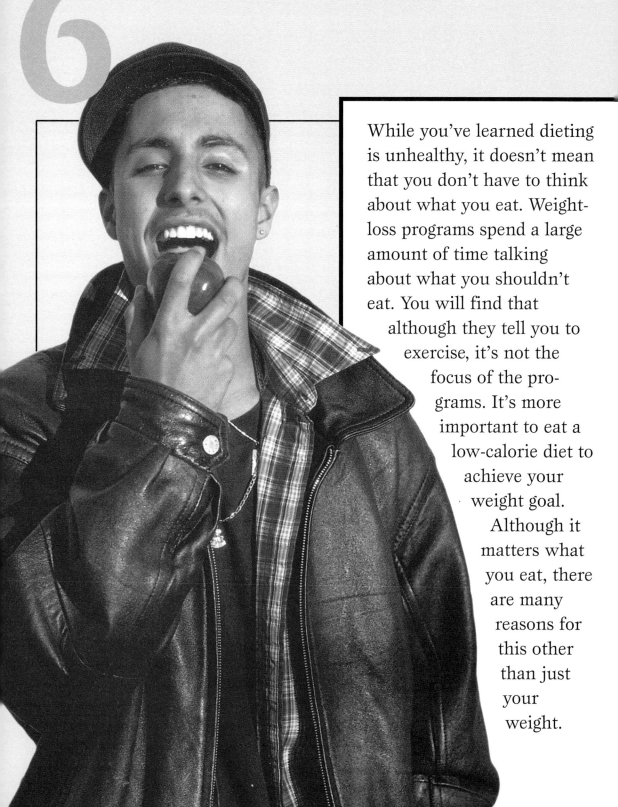

While you've learned dieting is unhealthy, it doesn't mean that you don't have to think about what you eat. Weight-loss programs spend a large amount of time talking about what you shouldn't eat. You will find that although they tell you to exercise, it's not the focus of the pro-grams. It's more important to eat a low-calorie diet to achieve your weight goal. Although it matters what you eat, there are many reasons for this other than just your weight.

Eating nutritious foods and exercising regularly is all you have to do to keep your weight at a level that is natural and right for you. As long as you do this, you may find that those weight-loss programs don't have a place in your life.

What Is the Right Amount of Exercise?

The Centers for Disease Control and Prevention (CDC) and the American Council on Sports Medicine recommend that a person get "about thirty minutes of moderate exercise on most days of the week." Michael Pratt, the physical activity coordinator for the CDC, says that doesn't mean you have to go to extremes. In fact, exercise can get out of hand, as we learned earlier, in the form of compulsive exercise. The whole idea is that you should enjoy physical activity. It should not be a chore and you should not become obsessed with it.

Make Exercise Fun

When you make exercise enjoyable, and not something you do to lose weight, you are more likely to stick with it. You can become frustrated and discouraged about exercising if you are using it only to lose weight. When you don't see the results you want, you may totally give it up. But there are so many other benefits to exercise. First, it releases endorphins (the body's natural painkillers), which automatically make you feel good. Exercise gives you energy and makes you feel more comfortable in your body. It reduces stress and makes you feel more self-confident.

What Kind of Exercise Is Right for Me?

You can try many different types of activity before you find what you like. Try a different activity on different days. The important thing is to enjoy it. This can mean taking a bike ride or going hiking with friends. It can mean a brisk walk in the morning and in the evening. Ask a friend to come along. You can motivate each other. When there is a choice between taking the stairs or the escalator, take the stairs. Instead of driving or being driven somewhere, walk or ride your bike there, if it's not far.

You could join a sport at school or start your own club. If you like to skate inline, start a hockey team. Offer to coach your younger sister's soccer team. As long as you're moving, you can do anything you want. If you change your goals about exercise and make it about having fun and staying fit instead of losing weight, you'll feel more satisfied.

What Foods Are Good for My Body?

It's not easy to eat right all the time. People eat what's convenient and easy because of busy schedules and

Exercise becomes easier and more fun when you focus on enjoying yourself, rather than on losing weight.

fast-paced lives. Sometimes parents aren't around to make sure you're eating a balanced meal. Sometimes school lunches aren't very appealing. But it's important to give a growing body plenty of fruits, vegetables, and protein. You should also avoid too much sugar, salt, and caffeine.

You have probably seen or heard about the four basic food groups. This idea was developed in the 1950s by the U.S. Department of Agriculture to try to help people choose the right foods. It's a simple, smart plan, and its guidelines still apply today.

The four basic groups are: milk and dairy products; meat, fish, and poultry; fruits and vegetables; and grains. You need food from all four groups to be healthy. Let's take a closer look at each one.

Milk and Dairy Products

Milk and other dairy products—such as yogurt, cheese, and ice cream—are excellent sources of calcium. Calcium helps your bones grow and stay strong, and it keeps teeth healthy. As your body continues to grow, calcium is an important part of staying healthy, especially for young women. It's recommended that teens have at least two servings of calcium every day, or 1,200 milligrams per day. Another good source of calcium is calcium-fortified orange juice. The vitamin C in the juice helps your body absorb the calcium.

Meat, Fish, and Poultry

Lean meats, fish, and poultry are good sources of protein. Protein is important because it helps to take care of your body tissue. Red meat is also an excellent source of iron. Iron helps your body deliver oxygen to body tissues. Strong body tissue gives your body the energy it needs, protects you from disease, and ensures that wounds heal properly. It is recommended that you eat four to six ounces of meat each day, or its equivalent.

If you are a vegetarian and cut out all meat from your diet, it's important to be sure you're getting enough protein. It is best to see a doctor regularly to make sure you are getting the necessary nutrients. A doctor may recommend a multivitamin if he or she doesn't think you are getting the proper nutrients. Nutritionists recommend eating plenty of beans, soy products, eggs, and peanut butter for protein. Tofu is also an excellent and healthy source of iron.

Fruits and Vegetables

Fruits and vegetables provide you with fiber, vitamins, and carbohydrates. Fiber helps cleanse your digestive system, and complex carbohydrates give you lots of energy. Many leafy, green vegetables are excellent sources of calcium as well. It is recommended that you eat at least four servings every day.

Grains

Grains include breads and cereals—such as bagels, whole grain breads, rice, pasta, and oats—and consist mainly of carbohydrates. They also give your body vitamins, minerals, and fiber. It is recommended that you eat at least four servings each day.

Another way to eat healthful foods is to eat fresh foods. When the food you eat is processed, many chemicals and additives are added to it. These kinds of foods often don't provide the nutrients your body needs. The next time you go to the grocery store, pay attention to the ingredients listed on the foods you buy. The first ingredient listed is the main ingredient. In other words, if you see "high fructose corn syrup" listed first on your fruit juice, it means the drink consists mostly of sugar. It may actually contain very little juice. Many packaged foods, such as TV dinners, contain a lot of sodium (salt). Foods manufactured by many weight-loss programs often use extra salt to add flavor. Too much salt can drain your body of calcium and can cause high blood pressure and water retention.

Two other products to watch out for are alcohol and caffeine. Not only is alcohol illegal for anyone under twenty-one years of age, it also can drain your body of essential vitamins and nutrients. Caffeine, found in chocolate, coffee, tea, and soda, can dehydrate the body. At first, it may seem as if caffeine is good because it gives you an energy boost, but in the end, it can make you more tired.

Eating Healthful Foods

It's not easy to follow all those food guidelines, especially when school, work, and social activities can get in the way. You may decide that you need some help in creating a meal plan that works best for you, and one that fits your lifestyle. Your doctor can certainly provide you with information, but you may get the most useful information from a registered dietitian.

A registered dietitian has a college degree and experience in the field of nutrition. He or she also has passed

A growing body needs foods from all four food groups: milk and dairy products; meat, fish, and poultry; fruits and vegetables; and grains.

a national examination and is registered with the American Dietetic Association (ADA). A person called a "nutritionist" does not have to follow these requirements and regulations. Getting the correct information about food and health is extremely important. The Nutrition Hotline of the American Dietetic Association is listed in the Where to Go for Help section at the end of this book. You can also contact your local health department for more information about nutrition.

Overall, the most important thing to remember is that eating right is good for your body. Good food makes you feel better, gives you more energy, helps you get a good night's sleep, and keeps everything functioning in your body. That doesn't mean you can never have any foods with sugar, salt, or caffeine. Most dietitians will tell you that it's a matter of moderation. A balanced diet is a flexible one. It doesn't make anything completely off-limits. But you'd be surprised how much better you feel when you eat foods that are filled with vitamins and nutrients!

A Final Word

Making changes isn't easy. The way you feel about food and your body is influenced by many factors in your life. It's complicated to sort through all those feelings and have an objective view of food, weight, and self-image. But food is a necessary part of life. Ellyn Satter, author of *Child of Mine: Eating with Love and Good Sense*, offers a definition of normal eating that may help you develop positive eating habits. She says, "Normal eating is flexible. It varies in response to your hunger, your schedule, your proximity to food, and your feelings. Normal eating takes up some of your time and attention, but keeps its place as only one important area of your life."

The lessons and habits you learn now will help you keep a positive attitude about food and weight for the rest of your life.

Glossary

anorexia nervosa Eating disorder in which a person eats very little or not at all.

binge eating When a person eats an excessively large amount of food at one sitting.

bulimia nervosa Eating disorder in which a person eats a very large amount of food and then removes it from his or her body by vomiting, extreme dieting, or abusing diet pills or laxatives.

endorphin A substance in the brain that can relieve pain and promote a sense of well-being.

fen-phen A combination of the drugs fenfluramine and phentermine; formerly used in some weight-loss programs.

metabolism The process by which the body uses food to produce energy.

portion control Practice that requires a person to eat a specified amount of different types of food.

purge To remove food from your body, such as through self-induced vomiting.

Redux Brand name for the drug dexfenfluramine; formerly used by some weight-loss programs.

set point The weight to which a person's body will naturally go when he or she is eating healthily and exercising regularly.

willpower The ability to control one's own actions.

yo-yo dieting Repeatedly going on and off one or more diets.

Where to Go for Help

American Dietetic Association
216 West Jackson Boulevard
Chicago, IL 60606-6995
(312) 899-0040
Nutrition Hotline
(800) 366-1655
Web site: http://www.eatright.org

Eating Disorders Awareness and Prevention, Inc. (EDAP)
603 Stewart Street, Suite 803
Seattle, WA 98101
(206) 382-3587
Web site: http://members.aol.com/edapinc

National Association of Anorexia Nervosa and Associated Disorders (ANAD)
Highland Hospital
Highland Park, IL 60035
(708) 432-8000
Web site: http://www.members.aol.com/
anad20/index.html

National Association to Advance Fat Acceptance (NAAFA)
Department GS
P. O. Box 188620
Sacramento, CA 95818
(916) 443-0303

In Canada

Anorexia Nervosa and Associated Disorders (ANAD)
109 - 2040 West 12th Avenue
Vancouver, BC V6J 2G2
(604) 739-2070

The National Eating Disorders Information Centre
CW 1, 304 - 200 Elizabeth Street
Toronto, ON M5G 2C4
(416) 340-4156

For Further Reading

Crook, Marion. *Looking Good: Teenagers and Eating Disorders.* Toronto: NC Press, Ltd., 1992.

Douglas, Susan J. *Where the Girls Are: Growing Up Female with the Mass Media.* New York: Random House, 1994.

Fraser, Laura. *Losing It: America's Obsession with Weight and the Industry That Feeds on It.* New York: Dutton Books, 1996.

Freedman, R. *Bodylove: Learning to Like Our Looks and Ourselves.* New York: HarperCollins, 1988.

Kaufman, Gershen, and Lev Raphael. *Stick Up for Yourself: Every Kid's Guide to Personal Power and Positive Self-Esteem.* Minneapolis: Free Spirit Publishing, Inc., 1990.

Lambert-Lagace, Louise. *The Nutrition Challenge for Women: Now You Don't Have to Diet to Stay Healthy and Fit.* Palo Alto, CA: Bull Publishing Co., 1990.

Larson, Roberta. *The American Dietetic Association's Complete Food and Nutrition Guide.* Chicago: Chronimed Publishing, 1996.

Index

About the Author

Michele I. Drohan is an editor and writer living in New York City.

Design and Layout: Christine Innamorato

Photo Credits

Photo on p. 21 by Ira Fox; p. 23 © Arthur Tilly/FPG International; p. 33 © Stephen Whalen/Viesti Associates, Inc.; p. 44 by Victor Englebert; p. 53 © Frank Siteman/Viesti Associates, Inc.; p. 57 © Eric Pearle/FPG International; All other photos by John Bentham.